Contents

Introduction

The Saxon Homeschool Testing Book for Intermediate 4 contains Tests, a Testing Schedule, Test Answer Forms, a Test Analysis Form, and Answers. Descriptions of these components are provided below.

About the Tests

The tests are available after every five lessons, beginning after lesson 10. The tests are designed to provide students with sufficient time to learn and practice each concept before they are assessed. The test design allows students to display the skills they have developed, and it fosters confidence that will benefit students when they encounter comprehensive standardized tests.

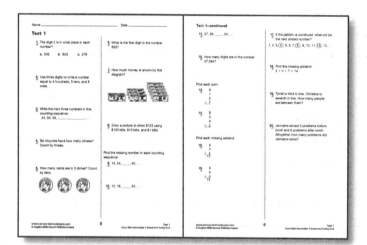
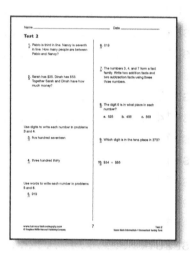

Testing Schedule

Administering the tests according to the schedule is essential. Each test is written to follow a specific five-lesson interval in the textbook. Following the schedule allows students sufficient practice on new topics before they are assessed on those topics.

Tests should be given after every fifth lesson, beginning after Lesson 10. The testing schedule is explained in greater detail on page 4 of this book.

Optional Test Answer Forms are included in this book. Each form provides a structure for students to show their work.

About the Test Answer Forms

This book contains three kinds of answer forms for the tests that you might find useful. These answer forms provide sufficient space for students to record their work on tests.

Answer Form A

This is a double-sided master with a grid background and partitions for recording the solutions to twenty problems.

Answer Form B

This is a double-sided master with a plain, white background and partitions for recording the solutions to twenty problems.

Answer Form C

This is a single-sided master with partitions for recording the solutions to twenty problems and a separate answer column on the right-hand side.

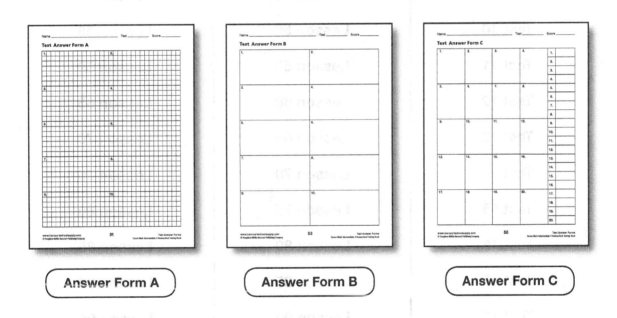

Answer Form A   Answer Form B   Answer Form C

Answers

The Answers are designed to be representative of students' work. Please keep in mind that problems may have more than one correct solution. We have attempted to stay as close as possible to the methods and procedures outlined in the textbook.

Testing Schedule

Test to be administered:	Covers material through	Give after teaching
Test 1	Lesson 5	Lesson 10
Test 2	Lesson 10	Lesson 15
Test 3	Lesson 15	Lesson 20
Test 4	Lesson 20	Lesson 25
Test 5	Lesson 25	Lesson 30
Test 6	Lesson 30	Lesson 35
Test 7	Lesson 35	Lesson 40
Test 8	Lesson 40	Lesson 45
Test 9	Lesson 45	Lesson 50
Test 10	Lesson 50	Lesson 55
Test 11	Lesson 55	Lesson 60
Test 12	Lesson 60	Lesson 65
Test 13	Lesson 65	Lesson 70
Test 14	Lesson 70	Lesson 75
Test 15	Lesson 75	Lesson 80
Test 16	Lesson 80	Lesson 85
Test 17	Lesson 85	Lesson 90
Test 18	Lesson 90	Lesson 95
Test 19	Lesson 95	Lesson 100
Test 20	Lesson 100	Lesson 105
Test 21	Lesson 105	Lesson 110
Test 22	Lesson 110	Lesson 115
Test 23	Lesson 115	Lesson 120

Test 1

1. The digit 2 is in what place in each
(4) number?

    a. 532   **b.** 823   **c.** 279

2. Use three digits to write a number
(4) equal to 4 hundreds, 3 tens, and 8
ones.

3. Write the next three numbers in this
(3) counting sequence:

    24, 30, 36, _____, _____, _____, ...

4. Six tricycles have how many wheels?
(3) Count by threes.

5. How many cents are in 3 dimes? Count
(3) by tens.

6. What is the first digit in the number
(3) 852?

7. How much money is shown by this
(4) diagram?

8. Draw a picture to show $123 using
(4) $100 bills, $10 bills, and $1 bills.

Find the missing number in each counting
sequence:

9. 16, 24, _____, 40, ...
(3)

10. 12, 18, _____, 30, ...
(3)

© Houghton Mifflin Harcourt Publishing Company

Test 1—continued

11. 27, 36, _____, 54, …
(3)

12. How many digits are in the number
(3) 27,394?

Find each sum:

13.   9
(1)   1
            2
         $+\ 7$

14.   8
(1)   3
            6
         $+\ 2$

Find each missing addend:

15.   5
(1)   n
         $+\ 2$
         ___
           11

16.   3
(1)   6
         $+\ n$
         ___
           13

17. If the pattern is continued, what will be
(3) the next circled number?

1, 2, 3, ④, 5, 6, 7, ⑧, 9, 10, 11, ⑫, 13, …

18. Find the missing addend:
(2) $2 + n + 7 = 14$

19. Tyrrell is third in line. Christina is
(5) seventh in line. How many people
are between them?

20. Jermaine solved 3 problems before
(1) lunch and 6 problems after lunch.
Altogether, how many problems did
Jermaine solve?

Name _____   Date _____

Test 2

1. Pablo is third in line. Nancy is seventh
(5) in line. How many people are between
Pablo and Nancy?

2. Sarah has $35. Dinah has $53.
(8) Together Sarah and Dinah have how
much money?

Use digits to write each number in problems
3 and **4**.

3. five hundred seventeen
(7)

4. three hundred thirty
(7)

Use words to write each number in problems
5 and **6**.

5. 919
(7)

6. 619
(7)

7. The numbers 3, 4, and 7 form a fact
(6) family. Write two addition facts and
two subtraction facts using these
three numbers.

8. The digit 6 is in what place in each
(4) number?

   a. 625   **b.** 456   **c.** 563

9. Which digit is in the tens place in 273?
(4)

10. $34 + $55
(8)

www.harcourtschoolsupply.com
© Houghton Mifflin Harcourt Publishing Company

Test 2–continued

11. $7 + 1 + 6 + 9 + 4 + 3$
(1)

12. $\begin{array}{r} 13 \\ -\ 6 \\ \end{array}$
(6)

13. $\begin{array}{r} 17 \\ -\ 8 \\ \end{array}$
(6)

14. $\begin{array}{r} 36 \\ +\ 29 \\ \end{array}$
(9)

Find each missing addend:

15. $\begin{array}{r} 7 \\ n \\ +\ 2 \\ \hline 12 \\ \end{array}$
(2)

16. $\begin{array}{r} 3 \\ 8 \\ +\ n \\ \hline 18 \\ \end{array}$
(2)

17. Write a number sentence for this picture:
(1)

Write the next three numbers in each counting sequence:

18. 9, 12, 15, ____, ____, ____, ...
(3)

19. 24, 21, 18, ____, ____, ____, ...
(3)

20. Which of these numbers is an even number?
(10)

A. 253   **B.** 352

C. 325   **D.** 523

Test 3

1. Sixty-three students sat on one side of
(1, 7) the cafeteria. Thirty students sat on the
other side. How many students were
there in all in the cafeteria?

2. Use digits to write the number three
(7) hundred fifty-two.

3. Use words to write the number 429.
(7)

4. Use digits and a comparison symbol
(Inv. 1) to write "Seven is greater than three."

5. The numbers 3, 7, and 10 form a fact
(6) family. Write two addition facts and
two subtraction facts using these
three numbers.

6. Is 572 an odd number or an even
(10) number?

7. Ramsey held 5 coins in his left hand
(11) and some more coins in his right hand.
Altogether, Ramsey had 12 coins in
his hands. How many coins were in
Ramsey's right hand?

8. To what number is the arrrow pointing?
(Inv. 1)

Compare:

9. 437 ◯ 374
(Inv. 1)

10. 562 ◯ 652
(Inv. 1)

Test 3–continued

Find the missing number in each counting sequence:

11. 48, _____, 56, 60, ...
₍₃₎

12. 27, _____, 21, 18, ...
₍₃₎

Find each missing number in problems **13** and **15.**

13.
₍₁₂₎
$$\begin{array}{r} 16 \\ -\ a \\ \hline 7 \end{array}$$

14.
₍₁₂₎
$$\begin{array}{r} a \\ -\ 8 \\ \hline 9 \end{array}$$

15.
₍₂₎
$$\begin{array}{r} 5 \\ b \\ +\ 4 \\ \hline 14 \end{array}$$

16.
₍₁₃₎
$$\begin{array}{r} \$274 \\ +\ \$442 \\ \hline \end{array}$$

17. $34 - 21$
₍₁₄₎

18. $33 - 16$
₍₁₅₎

19. $8 + 6 + 9 + 3 + 1 + 2 + 4$
₍₁₎

20. How many digits are in the number
₍₃₎ 326,559?

Test 4

1. One hundred boats sailed on Tuesday.
(1) Three hundred boats sailed on
Wednesday. Five hundred boats sailed
on Thursday. How many boats sailed
in the three days?

2. Lina had $337. For winning the race,
(13) she was paid $208. Then how much
money did Lina have?

3. Write 409 in expanded form.
(16)

4. If it is evening, what time is shown by
(19) this clock?

5. What temperature is shown on this
(18) thermometer?

6. one hundred thirty ◯ one hundred
(Inv. 1) thirteen

7. 912 ◯ 921
(Inv. 1)

8. How long is this pencil?
(Inv. 2)

9. Round 62 to the nearest ten.
(20)

10. Round $8.75 to the nearest dollar.
(20)

11. Xavier is standing ninth in line. Yvette is
(5) sixteenth in the same line. How many people are between Xavier and Yvette?

12. On the first day Elsa found thirty-one
(11) seashells. On the second day she found some more seashells. If Elsa found seventy-three seashells in the two days, how many did she find on the second day?

13.
(17)
```
    46
    35
    27
 + 39
```

14.
(13)
```
  476
+ 285
```

15.
(15)
```
   $63
 − $36
```

Find each missing number in problems **16–18.**

16.
(16)
```
    a
 − 23
   56
```

17.
(14)
```
   31
 +  d
   59
```

18.
(16)
```
   44
 −  e
   24
```

19. $14 + 28 + 36 + 21 + G = 100$
(2)

20. How many Xs are in this pattern?
(3) Count by threes.

$$\times\times\times\times\times\times$$
$$\times\times\times\times\times\times$$
$$\times\times\times\times\times\times$$

Test 5

1. Joaquin had thirty-eight dollars. Then
(25) he spent twenty-one dollars. How many dollars did Joaquin have left?

2. All the students lined up in two equal
(10) rows. Which of the following could be the total number of students?

A. 27   **B.** 49   **C.** 16

3. Forty-three people sat in the front row,
(1) eighty-one people sat in the second row, and fifty-seven people sat in the third row. Altogether, how many people sat in the first three rows?

4. Each side of this square is 11 mm long.
(Inv. 2) What is the perimeter of the square?

11 mm

5. Find the missing numbers in this
(3) counting sequence:

9, 18, _____, _____, 45, _____, ...

6. One yard equals how many feet?
(Inv. 2)

7. Round 37 to the nearest ten.
(20)

8. Compare: 14 − 8 ◯ 12 − 5
(6, Inv.1)

9. If it is morning, what time is shown by
(19) this clock?

Test 5—continued

10. Which street is perpendicular to Spruce?
(23)

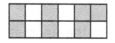

POPLAR	
SPRUCE	
GRAND	N / W—E / S

11. What fraction of this rectangle is shaded?
(22)

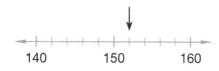

12. To what number is the arrow pointing?
(Inv. 1)

140   150   160

13. Which of these angles appears to be a right angle?
(23)

A.   B.   C.

Add, subtract, or find the missing number in problems **14–20.**

14. $8.62
(22)   + $3.59

15.   32
(15)   − 17

16.   q
(16)   − 36
          98

17.   532
(13)   + 227

18.   87
(14)   + f
          154

19.   985
(14)   − 143

20. 95 + 21 + 14 + 26 + 9
(17)

Test 6

1. Thirty crayons were in the box. Kadeeja
(25) took some crayons from the box.
Twenty-four crayons were left in the
box. How many crayons did Kadeeja
take from the box?

2. Thirty-eight boys sat in the first row.
(1) Forty-four boys sat in the second row.
Seventy boys sat in the third row.
Altogether, how many boys sat in the
first three rows?

3. The baseball glove costs forty-six
(11) dollars. Sherry has saved seventeen
dollars. How much more money
does Sherry need in order to buy the
baseball glove?

4. Use words to write the number 907.
(7,16)

5. Use digits and symbols to write "Eight
(Inv.1, times zero equals five times zero."
29)

6. Leon found this metal object in the
(Inv. 2) scrap yard. About how long is it?

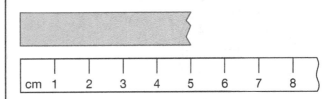

7. Draw a circle and shade $\frac{3}{4}$ of it.
(26)

8. Round $12.32 to the nearest dollar.
(20)

9. Find the missing numbers in this
(3) counting sequence:
48, ____, ____, 30, 24, ____, ...

10. What is the perimeter of this triangle?
(Inv. 2)

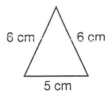

Test 6—continued

11. If it is evening, what time will it be in
(27) 2 hours and 15 minutes according to
this clock?

12. Change this addition problem to a
(27) multiplication problem:

$$7 + 7 + 7 + 7 + 7 + 7$$

13. The door is two meters tall. How many
(Inv. 2) centimeters is that?

14. Which product is greatest?
(29)
   A. 3×5 **B.** 5×6

   C. 9×5 **D.** 5×7

15. $860 - 240$
(14)

---

16. $\begin{array}{r} 76 \\ -\ 29 \\ \hline \end{array}$
(15)

17. $\begin{array}{r} 325 \\ +\ 869 \\ \hline \end{array}$
(13)

Find each missing number in problems
18 and **19**.

18. $\begin{array}{r} 36 \\ +\ t \\ \hline 87 \end{array}$
(14)

19. $\begin{array}{r} 87 \\ -\ p \\ \hline 43 \end{array}$
(16)

20. $4 + 3 + 6 + 5 + 2 + 3 + 7$
(1) $+ 2 + 8 + 9 + 1$

Test 7

1. It is one hundred twenty miles from
(11) Lillian's house to her grandmother's
house. Lillian has only driven fifteen
of those miles. How many miles does
Lillian have left to drive?

2. Use the digits 4, 8, and 7 once each
(10) to make an even number greater
than 800.

3. Draw a pattern of dots to show the
(Inv. 3) multiplication of 5 and 6.

4. Dara wrote her birth date as 5/14/99.
(5)
    a. In what month was Dara born?
    b. In what year was Dara born?

5. Draw two parallel lines.
(23)

6. This rectangle is 3 centimeters
(Inv. 3) long and 2 centimeters wide.
What is the area of the rectangle?

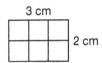

7. What fraction of this rectangle is
(22) shaded?

8. Change this addition
(27) problem to a multiplication
problem: 6 + 6 + 6 + 6 + 6

9. Round 46 to the nearest ten. Round
(20) 53 to the nearest ten. Then add the
rounded numbers.

10. Is the value of 4 nickels and 3 dimes
(10, 35) an even number of cents or an odd
number of cents?

Test 7–continued

11. *(Inv. 1)* The arrow is pointing to what number on this number line?

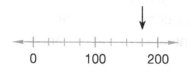

12. *(Inv. 3)*
a. 2×2
b. 7×7
c. 8×8

13. *(31)* Forty-five is how much less than fifty-four?

14. *(Inv. 3)* Find the square root:
$\sqrt{49}$

15. *(Inv. 1)* Compare: $43 + 56 \bigcirc 53 + 46$

Find each missing number. in problems **16** and **17**.

16. *(1)* $12 + w = 77$

17. *(16)*
$$\begin{array}{r} 747 \\ -\quad x \\ \hline 414 \end{array}$$

18. *(35)* Use words to write $4\frac{2}{3}$.

19. *(34)* Use digits to write six million.

20. *(30)*
$$\begin{array}{r} 846 \\ -\ 598 \\ \hline \end{array}$$

Test 8

1. Karim had two dimes, a quarter, and
(35) three pennies. Write this amount with
a dollar sign and decimal point.

2. Findlay is 182 miles west of
(11) Youngstown. Akron is 50 miles
west of Youngstown. How far is
it from Akron to Findlay?

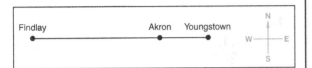

3. Name the fraction or mixed
(37) number marked by the
arrow on this number line:

4. Compare:
(Inv. 1) $12 + 24 + 45 \bigcirc 9 \times 9$

5. How many quarts of milk equal
(40) one gallon?

6. Use words to write 724,868.
(33)

7. Draw a circle and shade one sixth
(26) of it.

8. Use digits and symbols to compare
(7, Inv.1) eight hundred ninety-three and five
hundred ninety-two.

9. Which letter below has a right angle?
(23)

A L X W

10. What is the perimeter of a
(Inv. 2) rectangle that is 5 inches long and
3 inches wide?

11. Round 86 to the nearest ten.
(20) Round 84 to the nearest ten.
Add the rounded numbers.

12. If the diameter of a circle is two yards,
(Inv. 2, then the radius is how many feet?
21)

13. What mixed number is shown by
(35) the shaded rectangles?

14. $4.18 − $2.81
(30)

15. $\sqrt{81}$
(Inv. 3)

16. $485 + $357 + $53
(13)

17. a. $\begin{array}{r} 6 \\ \times\ 4 \\ \hline \end{array}$ **b.** $\begin{array}{r} 8 \\ \times\ 4 \\ \hline \end{array}$ **c.** $\begin{array}{r} 7 \\ \times\ 4 \\ \hline \end{array}$
(38)

Find each missing number in problems
18 and **19**.

18. $\begin{array}{r} e \\ +\ 243 \\ \hline 612 \end{array}$
(24)

19. $\begin{array}{r} y \\ -\ 412 \\ \hline 201 \end{array}$
(16)

20. $67 + 73 + 31 + 48 + n = 255$
(2)

Name _____ Date _____

Test 9

1. Six hundred fifty-five tickets were sold
(11) for the first performance of a play.
Altogether, nine hundred ninety-three
tickets were sold for two performances.
How many tickets were sold for the
second performance?

2. Benjamin paid $5.00 for an item that
(41) cost $4.73. How much money should
Benjamin get back?

3. Round 424 to the nearest hundred.
(42)

4. Draw and shade circles to show the
(35) mixed number $3\frac{1}{4}$.

5. Use words to write 12.4.
(Inv. 4)

6. It is morning. What time was it
(27) 1 hour 45 minutes ago according
to this clock?

7. To the nearest quarter inch,
(39, 45) how long is segment *AB*?

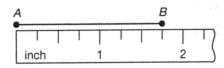

8. To what mixed number is the arrow
(37) pointing?

9. There were two hundred twenty-four
(31) cars on the highway. There were nine
hundred nine cars on the parkway.
How many more cars were on the
parkway?

Find each missing number in problems
10–12.

10. $\begin{array}{r} n \\ -\ 312 \\ \hline 527 \end{array}$
(24)

11. $\begin{array}{r} 814 \\ -\ \ s \\ \hline 303 \end{array}$
(16)

© Houghton Mifflin Harcourt Publishing Company
Saxon Math Intermediate 4 Homeschool Testing Book

Test 9–continued

12. $4r = 36$
(41)

13. $\begin{array}{r} \$7.03 \\ - \$3.47 \\ \hline \end{array}$
(41)

14. $\begin{array}{r} 60 \\ \times\ 3 \\ \hline \end{array}$
(42)

15. $\begin{array}{r} 52 \\ \times\ 4 \\ \hline \end{array}$
(44)

16. $68 + (8 \times 4)$
(45)

17. $4 \times (2 + 6)$
(45)

18. $\$8.14 + 76¢ + \$2$
(43)

19. $0.75 - 0.50$
(43)

20. $\sqrt{49} + \sqrt{16}$
(Inv. 3)

www.harcourtschoolsupply.com
© Houghton Mifflin Harcourt Publishing Company

Test 10

1. Four hundred thirty-nine students
(1) are in one school. Seven hundred
thirty-eight students are in another
school. What is the total number of
students in the two schools?

2. Liza has three hundred seventeen
(31) coins in her collection. Tamca found
five hundred eighty-one coins in her
collection. Tamca has how many more
coins than Liza?

3. If the radius of a circle is 3 feet, then its
(Inv. 2, diameter is
21)

    A. 6 yards   **B.** 2 yards

    C. $1\frac{1}{2}$ feet   **D.** 9 feet

4. Which digit in 12.3 is in the tenths
(50) place?

5. Use the digits 1, 2, 3, and 4 once each
(10) to write an odd number between 3300
and 3600.

6. Write the mixed number shown
(35) by the shaded circles.

7. What is the perimeter of this shape?
(Inv. 2) Dimensions are in feet.

8. The league has 6 teams with 9 players
(49) on each team. How many players does
the league have altogether?

9. Round 467 to the nearest hundred.
(42)

Add, subtract, multiply, or find the missing
number in problems **10–18**.

10.   73,804
(51) + 48,697

11. $8.50
(30) − $4.81

© Houghton Mifflin Harcourt Publishing Company

12.
(24)
$$
\begin{array}{r}
n \\
+\ 267 \\
\hline
912
\end{array}
$$

13.
(24)
$$
\begin{array}{r}
z \\
+\ 501 \\
\hline
1{,}452
\end{array}
$$

14.
(44)
$$
\begin{array}{r}
21 \\
\times\ 6 \\
\hline
\end{array}
$$

15.
(48)
$$
\begin{array}{r}
73 \\
\times\ 7 \\
\hline
\end{array}
$$

16. $4.36 - 2.4$
(50)

17. $4.3 + 2.64$
(50)

18. $\$3.46 + \$2 + 43¢ + 9¢$
(43)

19. Compare:
(Inv. 1, 45)
$(2 \times 3) + 4 \bigcirc 2 \times (3 + 4)$

20. a. $3\overline{)27}$ **b.** $18 \div 3$ **c.** $\dfrac{42}{6}$
(46)

Test 11

1. Forty-two days is how many weeks?
(52, 54)

2. List the factors of 15.
(55)

3. Forty books were put into eight equal
(52) stacks. How many books were in each stack?

4. Draw a circle and shade 25% of it.
(Inv. 5)

5. How many years are in five centuries?
(52, 54)

6. Find the seventh multiple of 6. Then
(55) subtract 12. What is the difference?

7. Compare: $\frac{1}{4}$ ◯ 50%
(Inv. 5)

8. Segment *DE* is 4 cm long.
(45) Segment *DF* is 12 cm long.
How long is segment *EF*?

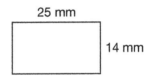

D   E   F

9. What is the perimeter of this rectangle?
(Inv. 2)

25 mm

14 mm

10. Round 5,280 to the nearest thousand.
(54)

11. $13.00
(41)   − $6.35

Test 11–continued

12.
(51)
$$73{,}129$$
$$+\ 8{,}293$$

13.
(52)
$$46{,}218$$
$$-\ 17{,}649$$

14.
(48)
$$79$$
$$\times\ \ 7$$

15. $3.47 + 2.6 + 12.4$
(50)

16. $\sqrt{25} + (20 \div 4)$
(Inv. 3, 45)

17. $52 \div 7$
(53)

18.
(30)
$$208$$
$$-\ 69$$

Find each missing number in problems **19** and **20**.

19.
(16)
$$n$$
$$-\ 351$$
$$\overline{600}$$

20.
(24)
$$z$$
$$+\ 853$$
$$\overline{1{,}172}$$

Name _____ Date _____

Test 12

1. Two thousand, eight hundred fourteen
(31) is how much greater than one
    thousand, five hundred ninety-six?

2. How many people could ride in
(49) thirty-five carts if seven people
    could ride in each cart?

3. Dora rode her bike 5 miles to her
(60) grandmother's house. The ride took
    30 minutes. On average, how many
    minutes did it take Dora to ride
    each mile?

4. The Thatcher family ate 25 apples in
(60) 5 days. On average, how many apples
    did the Thatchers eat each day?

5. Andreas drove for 8 hours at an
(57) average speed of 45 miles per hour.
    How far did Andreas drive?

6. What fraction of this rectangle is
(22) shaded?

7. Ten decades is the same as how
(54) many centuries?

8. Compare these fractions. Draw and
(56) shade two congruent circles to show
    the comparison.

$$\frac{2}{3} \bigcirc \frac{3}{4}$$

9. Estimate the sum of 487 and 229 by
(42, 59) rounding each number to the nearest
    hundred before adding.

10. Which segment in this circle is a
(45) diameter?

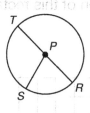

11. Find the eighth multiple of six. Then
(55) subtract 28. What is the difference?

12. $71.43
(22) + $16.77

13. 86,791
(52) − 47,802

14. 6.48 − (1.6 + 2.44)
(45, 50)

15. 1,000 − (12 × 8)
(45)

16. 760
(58) × 5

17. 377
(58) × 3

18. $\sqrt{36} \div 6$
(Inv.3, 46)

19. 4)̄31
(53)

20. Find the missing factor: $9r = 63$
(41)

Name _____ Date _____

Test 13

1. Carole took 6 big steps to measure
(Inv. 2) the width of the room. If each step
was one yard, then the width of the
room was how many feet?

2. Every third bead on Mary's necklace is
(52) red. There are one hundred fifty-three
beads in all. How many beads are red?

3. Two-fifths of the students walked to
(61) school. What fraction of the students
did not walk to school?

4. Compare: 25% of 24 ◯ 3 × 2
(Inv. 5)

5. What is the area of this square?
(Inv. 3)

 12 mm

6. Estimate the product of 79 and 9.
(59)

7. Chris' car could go 28 miles on one
(57) gallon of gas. How far could Chris' car
go on seven gallons of gas?

8. Name the polygon.
(63)

9. If each side of the polygon in problem
(Inv. 2) 8 measures 3 units, then what is its
perimeter?

10. Compare. Draw and shade two
(56) congruent rectangles to show the
comparison.

$\frac{1}{4}$ ◯ $\frac{2}{5}$

11. If 27% of the students were boys,
(Inv. 5) then what percent of the students
were girls?

12. 37,394 + 117,087
(51)

13. $11 − 9¢
(50)

14. 5 × 8 × 4
(62)

15. $3^2 + 8^2$
(62)

16. 374
(58) × 6

17. 7)‾322‾
(65)

18. 32 ÷ (20 ÷ 5)
(45, 47)

19. 7.4 + 3.84 + 12.5
(50)

20. Find the missing factor: $4r = 52$
(41, 64)

Test 14

1. Ami and Michelle had 96 fence posts.
(70) They used one fourth of the posts for
the garden and the rest for their yard.
How many posts did Ami and Michelle
use for the garden?

2. Thirty-five percent of the lights in the
(Inv. 5) house were on. What percent of the
lights were off?

3. Each bagel contains an average of
(49) seven raisins. How many raisins are
in 105 bagels?

4. Estimate the sum of 5,879 and 7,215
(42, 59) by rounding each number to the
nearest thousand before adding.

5. What is the value of 7 pennies,
(35) 2 dimes, 5 quarters, and 7 nickels?
Write the answer using a dollar sign
and decimal point.

6. One-fifth of the salespeople
(70) earned a commission. There were
60 salespeople in all. How many
salespeople earned a commission?

7. What number is indicated on the
(Inv. 1) number line below?

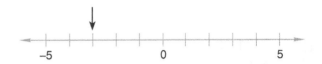

8. Douglas has a pentagon and an
(63) octagon. What is the total number
of sides on the two polygons?

9. a. The line segment shown below
(69)   is how many centimeters long?

   b. The segment is how many
       millimeters long?

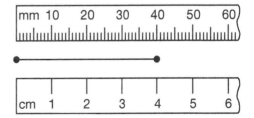

10. What is the perimeter of the rectangle?
(Inv. 2)

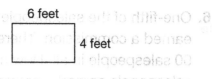

6 feet

4 feet

11. What is the area of the rectangle in
(Inv. 3) problem **10**?

12. $421.90
(22)   + $209.26

13. $30.00
(41)   − $29.59

14. $3.13
(58)   ×   4

15. 24 × 20
(67)

16. $4^2 − \sqrt{4}$
(Inv 3,
62)

17. 279 ÷ 4
(68)

18. 3 × 7 × 8
(62)

19. 5.16 − 3.8
(50)

20. Find the missing factor: $6s = 96$
(41, 64)

Test 15

1. Shannon has six days to read a
(52) 300-page book. If she wants to read
the same number of pages each
day, how many pages should Shannon
read each day?

2. When Shannon has read three-fifths
(61) of the book, what fraction will she still
have left to read?

Use the information given below to answer
problems **3–5**.

*Eighty students voted for their favorite
foods. Thirty-two voted for pizza. Hot
dogs received eight fewer votes than
pizza. The remaining students voted
for hamburgers.*

3. How many students chose hot dogs
(72) as their favorite food?

4. How many students chose hamburgers
(72) as their favorite food?

5. Which food received the most votes?
(72)

6. How many days equal nine weeks?
(49)

7. In the word HIPPOPOTAMI, what
(74) fraction of the letters are Os?

8. Mary ran a 5-kilometer race. Five
(Inv. 2) kilometers is how many meters?

9. Takeshi entered a 10-kilometer race but
(70) walked one fifth of the distance. How
many kilometers did Takeshi walk?

10. What is the perimeter of this triangle?
(Inv. 2,
69)

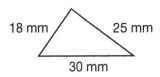

11. The length of $\overline{AB}$ is 42 mm. The length
(45) of $\overline{AC}$ is 74 mm. What is the length
of $\overline{BC}$?

12. $27 − ($24.17 − 58¢)
(45, 50)

13. 44,317 − 672
(52)

14. 3.4 + 2.76 + 0.23 + 2.5
(50)

15. $4.91 × 7
(58)

16. $6\overline{)341}$
(68)

17. $6\overline{)545}$
(71)

Find each missing number in problems
18 and **19.**

18. $4a = 240$
(41)

19.
(24)

$$\begin{array}{r} 374 \\ 215 \\ +\quad n \\ \hline 958 \end{array}$$

20. Compare: 2×5^2 $\bigcirc$ $\sqrt{81} \times \sqrt{16}$
(Inv. 3, 62)

© Houghton Mifflin Harcourt Publishing Company

Test 16

1. Miguel faces east and then turns
(75) 90° clockwise. What direction is
Miguel facing after the turn?

    A. north   **B.** south

    C. east   **D.** west

2. Nectarines cost 57¢ per pound. What
(57) is the price for 4 pounds of nectarines?

3. In darts, the sum of Julie's score
(72) and José's score was equal to
Johnna's score. If Johnna's score
was 91 and José's score was 37,
what was Julie's score?

4. One-eighth of the 96 delegates
(70) were assigned to each room. How
many delegates were assigned to
each room?

5. Draw a triangle congruent to this
(79) triangle. Then draw its line of
symmetry.

6. What fraction of the letters in the word
(74) ALABAMA are not As?

7. The truck weighs 2 tons. How many
(77) pounds is 2 tons?

8. Which is the more reasonable measure
(77) of weight for a box of cereal?

    A. 300 g   **B.** 300 kg

9. Which triangle appears to be an
(78) equilateral triangle?

  A.   **B.**

  C.   **D.**

10. Seventy-five thousand, twenty-one
(31, 34) dollars is how much greater than
sixty-four thousand, nine hundred
fifty-seven dollars?

11. Estimate the sum of 287 and 708.
(59)

16. 4)3,228
(80)

12. Lowell could paint 12 signs in 2 hours.
(52) How many signs could Lowell paint in 1 hour?

17. 4,321 ÷ 5
(76)

Find each missing number in problems **18** and **19.**

13. 5,963 − (409 × 6)
(45)

18. 287 = 7k
(41)

14. $7.97 × 7
(58)

19. 4,642
(24)   1,391
      +   h
     8,237

15. 64.8 + 2.17
(50)

20. Use a symbol to compare the number
(40) of cups in 1 pint to the number of cups in 1 quart.

© Houghton Mifflin Harcourt Publishing Company

Test 17

1. It takes Kylie 30 minutes to ride her bike to work. At what time should Kylie start riding her bike to work if she wants to arrive at 12:05 p.m.?
(27)

5. Tansu bought a rectangular lot that was 6 miles long and 4 miles wide. Half of the land was wetlands. How many square miles of land was wetlands?
(Inv. 3, 70)

2. Jennifer can walk one mile in 15 minutes. At that rate how far can she walk in an hour?
(57)

6. Which angle appears to be a 90° angle?
(81)

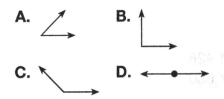

3. Bertrand rented 3 DVDs for $3.97 each. The sales tax was 89¢.
(83)

   a. What was the total price?

   b. If Bertrand paid with a $20 bill, how much change did he get back?

7. Round seven thousand, four hundred ninety-six to the nearest thousand.
(42, 59)

Use the information given in this bar graph to answer problem **4**.

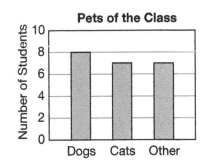

8. Three pounds is how many ounces?
(77)

9. One-third of the 18 flowers are roses. How many flowers are roses?
(70)

4. How many students have dogs or cats as pets?
(Inv. 6)

10. Write $\frac{435}{1000}$ as a decimal number.
(84)

11. Write 0.321 as a fraction.
(84)

12.
(22)
$$\begin{array}{r} \$47.36 \\ + \ \$ \ 9.86 \\ \hline \end{array}$$

13.
(43)
$$\begin{array}{r} 31.428 \\ + \ 17.680 \\ \hline \end{array}$$

14.
(58)
$$\begin{array}{r} 621 \\ \times \quad 7 \\ \hline \end{array}$$

15. 100×27
(85)

16. $7\overline{)\$6.37}$
(76)

17. $2{,}100 \div (12 \div 4)$
(45)

Find each missing number in problems **18** and **19.**

18. $7m = 560$
(41)

19.
(2)
$$\begin{array}{r} 6 \\ 14 \\ n \\ 17 \\ 25 \\ + \ 110 \\ \hline 200 \end{array}$$

20.
(67)
$$\begin{array}{r} 67 \\ \times \quad 30 \\ \hline \end{array}$$

© Houghton Mifflin Harcourt Publishing Company

Name _____   Date _____

Test 18

1. Four quarters, 3 dimes, 2 nickels, and
(35) 1 penny is how much money?

2. Nia put 50 math books as evenly
(88) as possible in 7 stacks.

    a. How many stacks had exactly
       7 books?

    b. How many stacks had 8 books?

3. Zelda paid one dollar for some gum
(83) and received 27¢ back in change.
How much did the gum cost?

4. Janet called each of her five brothers
(49) 7 times. In all how many calls did
Janet make?

5. Round 6,348 to the nearest thousand.
(59) Round 1,863 to the nearest thousand.
Find the sum of the two rounded
numbers.

6. Which two sides of this pentagon
(23) appear to be parallel?

7. Draw a polygon congruent to the
(79) polygon in problem 6. Then draw its
line of symmetry.

8. A square with a perimeter of 64 mm
(Inv. 2) has sides that are how many
millimeters long?

9. Segment *AB* is 14 mm long. Segment
(45) *BC* is 22 mm long. Segment *AD* is
76 mm long. How long is segment *CD*?

10. Draw and shade circles to show that
(89) $1\frac{1}{2}$ equals $\frac{3}{2}$.

www.harcourtschoolsupply.com
© Houghton Mifflin Harcourt Publishing Company

Test 18
Saxon Math Intermediate 4 Homeschool Testing Book

Test 18–continued

11.
(22)
$$\$ 52.28$$
$$+ \$249.71$$

12.
(52)
$$29{,}268$$
$$- \quad 9{,}819$$

13.
(85)
$$\$6.32$$
$$\times \qquad 10$$

14.
(90)
$$36$$
$$\times 42$$

15.
(80)
$$4\overline{)\$32.08}$$

16.
(Inv. 3, 62)
$$6^2 - \sqrt{36}$$

17.
(50)
$$3.375 + 1.45$$

18.
(86)
$$800 \times 30$$

Find each missing number in problems **19** and **20**.

19.
(24)
$$n$$
$$+ \; 977$$
$$4{,}381$$

20.
(2)
$$3$$
$$6$$
$$9$$
$$20$$
$$7$$
$$+ \; n$$
$$61$$

© Houghton Mifflin Harcourt Publishing Company

Saxon Math Intermediate 4 Homeschool Testing Book

Test 19

1. In a board game, Grant scored four
(94) points more than Kobe. Kobe scored
three times as many points as Todd.
If Todd scored 6 points, how many
points did Grant score?

2. Draw a trapezoid.
(92)

3. The toll is $1.30. Pilar put four dimes
(94) and three nickels in the basket. How
much more money does she need to
put in the basket?

4. Thirty-three desks were arranged in
(88) 6 rows as evenly as possible.

   a. How many rows had exactly
   5 desks?

   b. How many rows had 6 desks?

5. Draw a rectangle and shade 75% of it.
(Inv. 5)

6. a. What decimal number names the
(Inv. 4) shaded part of this square?

   b. What decimal number names the
   part that is not shaded?

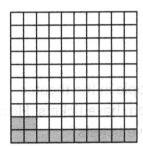

7. Which digit in 14.375 is in the
(91) hundredths place?

8. Estimate the product of 37 and 51.
(93) Then find the exact product.

9. Jane bought a meter of ribbon and cut
(69, 70) off about one-fifth of it to make a bow.
About how many millimeters of ribbon
did Jane use to make the bow?

Test 19–continued

10. What is the area of this rectangle?
(Inv. 3)

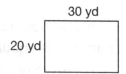

30 yd

20 yd

11. There are 18 people in the theater.
(95) Two-thirds of them have tickets. How many people have tickets?

12. Cedric drove 364 miles in 7 hours. If
(60) Cedric drove at a steady speed, how far did he drive in one hour?

13. Write $\frac{17}{100}$ as a decimal number.
(Inv. 4)

14. 2.3 − 0.23
(91)

15. 30 × 700
(86)

16. $8.16 × 9
(58)

17.   26
(90) x 42

18. 4)‾6‾0‾0‾
(80)

19. $\frac{732}{4}$
(76)

20. Find the missing addend:
(2) 2 + 5 + 6 + 9 + n + 5 + 2 + 2 + 1 = 49

Test 20

1. Five people were eating orange slices.
(96) Carol ate 3, April ate 6, Mai ate 7,
Patrick ate 7, and Santiago ate 2.
What was the average number of
orange slices eaten by each person?

2. Write $8\frac{3}{10}$ in decimal form.
(Inv. 4)

3. Which digit in 29.64 is in the same
(91) place as the 7 in 3.07?

4. Two-fifths of the 60 marchers were out
(95) of step. How many marchers were out
of step?

5. Compare:
(Inv. 3, 45) $(7^2 + 1) \div \sqrt{25} \bigcirc \sqrt{81}$

6. 24.5 − 6.27
(91)

7. a. What is the radius of the circle
(21, 69) below in millimeters?

   b. What is the diameter of the circle
   in centimeters?

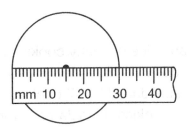

8. Write 9.31 using words.
(Inv. 4)

9. Estimate the product of 68 and 42.
(93)

10. Apples are priced at 39¢ per pound.
(57) What is the cost of 5 pounds of
apples?

11. Find the perimeter and area of this
(Inv. 2, Inv. 3) rectangle.

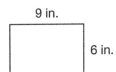

9 in.

6 in.

12. Find the sum of three hundred
(34, 51) sixty-three thousand, four hundred
fifty-two and eight thousand,
seven hundred forty-nine.

13. James has twice as many cookies as
(94) Josefina. Josefina has 4 fewer cookies
than Jamal. If Jamal has 7 cookies,
how many cookies does James have?

14. Draw circles to show that 3 equals $\frac{9}{3}$.
(89)

15. Something is wrong with the sign
(22) below. Draw two signs that show
different ways to correct the sign's
error.

SODAS
0.35¢
a can

16. What is the median of these scores?
(97) 90, 80, 75, 80, 90, 95, 100

17. Which word names this shape?
(98)

   A. cone
   B. cylinder
   C. sphere

18. 70 × 70
(86)

19.   73
(90) × 29

20. 3)$27.93
(76)

Name _____ Date _____

Test 21

Use the information given in the circle graph to answer problems **1–4**.

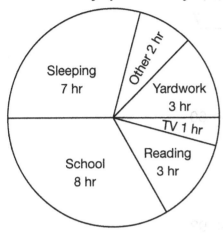

How Holly Spent Her Day

Sleeping 7 hr
Other 2 hr
Yardwork 3 hr
TV 1 hr
Reading 3 hr
School 8 hr

1. What is the total number of hours
(Inv. 6) shown in the graph?

2. What fraction of Holly's day was spent
(Inv. 6) sleeping?

3. If Holly starts school at 8:00 a.m., what
(Inv. 6) time does school end?

4. How many hours did Holly spend at
(Inv. 6) school and reading?

Use the information given below to answer problems **5** and **6**.

Samantha has 8 cats. Each cat eats $\frac{1}{2}$ can of food each day. Cat food costs 63¢ per can.

5. How many total cans of cat food are
(57) eaten each day?

6. How much does Samantha spend on
(57) cat food per day?

7. If the perimeter of a square is 88
(Inv. 2) centimeters, how long is each side of
the square?

8. Change the improper fraction $\frac{9}{4}$ to a
(104) mixed number.

Test 21—continued

9. What fraction name for 1 is shown by this rectangle?
(103)

10. Miriam bought three audiocasette tapes for $5.21 each. The sales tax was $1.17. She paid the clerk with a twenty-dollar bill. How much change should Miriam get back?
(83)

11. **a.** What is the length of the line segment in millimeters?
(102)
b. What is the length of the segment in centimeters?

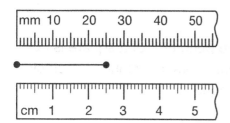

12. The freight train traveled 312 miles in 6 hours.
(57, 60)
a. The train's average rate was how many miles per hour?
b. At that rate, how far could the train go in 10 hours?

13. $45.00
(41) − $19.63

14. $3.66
(58) ×   7

15. 60×60
(86)

16. 46×92
(90)

17. $10\overline{)426}$
(105)

18. $960 \div 2^3$
(62, 80)

19. $4.2 - (3.2 + 0.63)$
(45, 91)

20. Find the missing number: 697
(16)   −   p
                                    ──────
                                        302

Test 22

Use the information given in this table to answer problems **1** and **2**.

Shipping Charges

Weight	Zone 1	Zone 2
Up to 4 pounds	$1.62	$1.82
4 pounds 1 ounce to 7 pounds	$1.86	$1.89
7 pounds 1 ounce or more	$2.01	$2.09

1. How much does it cost to ship a
(101)   4-pound package to Zone 2?

2. How much more does it cost to ship
(101)   a 9-pound package to Zone 2 than to Zone 1?

3. Three-eighths of the 80 tadpoles
(95)   already had back legs. How many tadpoles had back legs?

4. a. Find the length of this line segment
(102)   in millimeters.

 b. Find the length of the segment in centimeters.

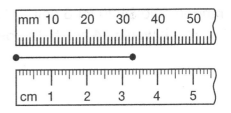

5. Find three fractions equivalent to
(109) $\frac{1}{3}$ by using $\frac{2}{2}$, $\frac{3}{3}$, and $\frac{4}{4}$ as multipliers.

6. Use words to write 574.6.
(Inv. 4)

7. Estimate the product of 396 and 48.
(59)

8. Change the improper fraction $\frac{8}{5}$ to a
(104)   mixed number.

Test 22–continued

9. Claudia put 25 marbles in a jar. How many marbles could Claudia put in 9 jars?
(49)

10. Brandon paid $4.80 for 6 golf balls. How much would 24 golf balls cost?
(72)

11. $14.00 − $7.65
(41)

12. 6.68 + 14.3 + 9.2
(50)

13. 12.7 − 3.46
(91)

14. $2^3 + \sqrt{64}$
(Inv. 3, 62)

15. 37 × 40
(67)

16. $\dfrac{324}{4}$
(65)

17. 436 ÷ 10
(105)

18. $40\overline{)123}$
(110)

19. What is the value of *bh* when *b* is 8 and *h* is 6?
(106)

20. What is the probability that a tossed coin will land tails up?
(Inv. 10)

Name _____   Date _____

Test 23

1. Tickets for the movie cost $7.25 for
(94) adults and $6.50 for students. Gailyn
bought tickets for two adults and four
students. Altogether, how much did
Gailyn pay?

2. Estimate the area of this triangle. Each
(111) small square represents one square
centimeter.

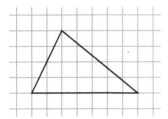

3. Two dimes equal what percent of
(Inv. 5) a dollar?

4. This rectangle is 5 cm long and 4 cm
(Inv.3, 70) wide. Half the rectangle is shaded.
What is the area of the shaded part
of the rectangle?

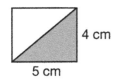

4 cm

5 cm

5. Complete the equivalent fraction:
(115) $\frac{3}{4} = \frac{?}{12}$

6. What fraction name for 1 has a
(103) denominator of 6?

7. Draw a picture to show that $\frac{1}{4}$ and
(109) $\frac{2}{8}$ are equivalent fractions

8. The champion bike rider could ride
(57) 56 miles in 2 hours. At the same
average speed, how far could she
ride in 6 hours?

9. The campers bought 2 sleeping bags
(83) for $39.99 each and a lantern for
$12.79. Sales tax was $5.24. They
paid for the items with a $100 bill.
How much change should they have
gotten back?

10. Eighty people stood in line. Six of them
(88) could ride in each van. If there were
only nine vans, how many people did
not get a ride?

11. $26.31 + 6.83 + 12.9$
(50)

12. $134.55 - 23.9$
(91)

13. $\frac{1}{7} + \frac{1}{7}$
(107)

14. $\frac{7}{8} - \frac{2}{8}$
(107)

15. $2\frac{1}{4} + 1\frac{3}{4}$
(114)

16. $\$1.25 \times 16$
(113)

17. $\$48.36 \div 4$
(80)

18. $\frac{672}{8}$
(65)

19. $40\overline{)640}$
(110)

20. Reduce:
(112)

   a. $\frac{3}{9}$ **b.** $\frac{2}{10}$ **c.** $\frac{9}{27}$

© Houghton Mifflin Harcourt Publishing Company
Saxon Math Intermediate 4 Homeschool Testing Book

Name _____   Test _____   Score _____

Test Answer Form A

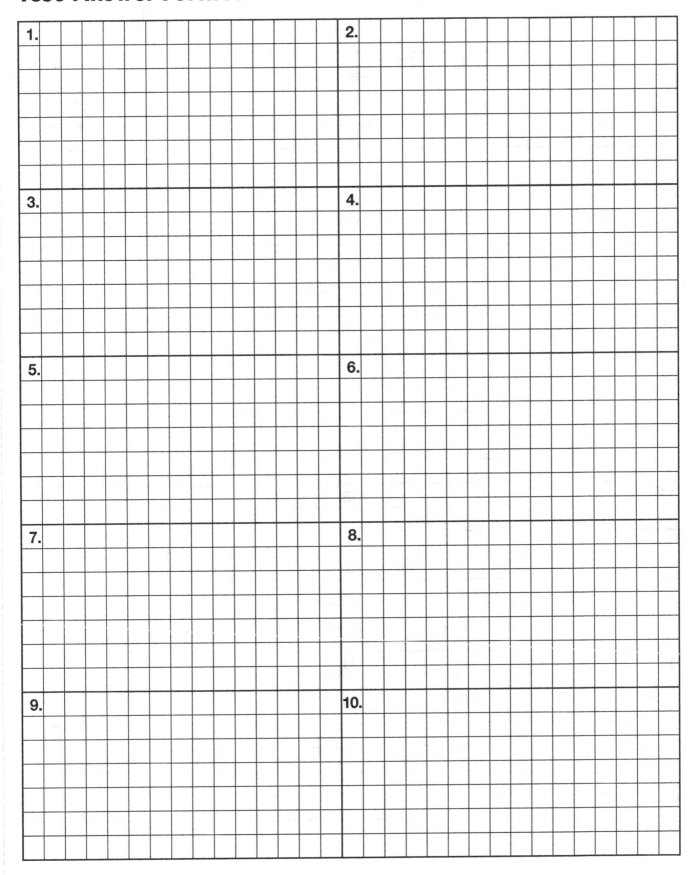

www.harcourtschoolsupply.com
© Houghton Mifflin Harcourt Publishing Company

Test Answer Forms
Saxon Math Intermediate 4 Homeschool Testing Book

Test Answer Form A–continued

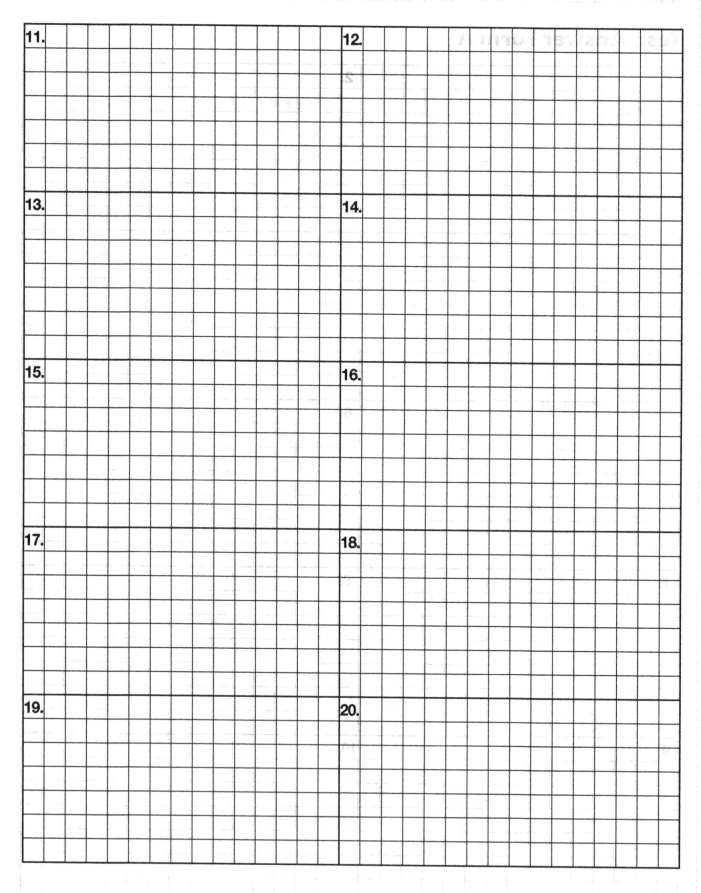

11.

12.

13.

14.

15.

16.

17.

18.

19.

20.

© Houghton Mifflin Harcourt Publishing Company

Test Answer Forms
Saxon Math Intermediate 4 Homeschool Testing Book

Name _____   Test _____   Score _____

Test Answer Form B

1.	2.
3.	4.
5.	6.
7.	8.
9.	10.

11.	**12.**
13.	**14.**
15.	**16.**
17.	**18.**
19.	**20.**

Name _____ Test _____ Score _____

Test Answer Form C

1.	2.	3.	4.	1.	
				2.	
				3.	
				4.	
5.	6.	7.	8.	5.	
				6.	
				7.	
				8.	
9.	10.	11.	12.	9.	
				10.	
				11.	
				12.	
13.	14.	15.	16.	13.	
				14.	
				15.	
				16.	
17.	18	19.	20.	17.	
				18.	
				19.	
				20.	

www.harcourtschoolsupply.com

© Houghton Mifflin Harcourt Publishing Company

55

Test Answer Forms

Saxon Math Intermediate 4 Homeschool Testing Book

Test Analysis Form

Test Item No.	Test Number											
	1	2	3	4	5	6	7	8	9	10	11	12
	Lesson Assessed											
1.	4	5	1, 7	1	25	25	11	35	11	1	52, 54	31
2.	4	8	7	13	10	1	10	11	41	31	55	49
3.	3	7	7	16	1	11	Inv. 3	37	42	Inv. 2, 21	52	60
4.	3	7	Inv. 1	19	Inv. 2	7, 16	5	Inv. 1	35	50	Inv. 5	60
5.	3	7	6	18	3	Inv. 1, 29	23	40	Inv. 4	10	52, 54	57
6.	3	7	10	Inv. 1	Inv. 2	Inv. 2	Inv. 3	33	27	35	55	22
7.	4	6	11	Inv. 1	20	26	22	26	39, 45	Inv. 2	Inv. 5	54
8.	4	4	Inv. 1	Inv. 2	6, Inv. 1	20	27	7, Inv. 1	37	49	45	56
9.	3	4	Inv. 1	20	19	3	20	23	31	42	Inv. 2	42, 59
10.	3	8	Inv. 1	20	23	Inv. 2	10, 35	Inv. 2	24	51	54	45
11.	3	1	3	5	22	27	Inv. 1	20	16	30	41	55
12.	3	6	3	11	Inv. 1	27	Inv. 3	Inv. 2, 21	41	24	51	22
13.	1	6	12	17	23	Inv. 2	31	35	41	24	52	52
14.	1	9	12	13	22	29	Inv. 3	30	42	44	48	45, 50
15.	1	2	2	15	15	14	Inv. 1	Inv. 3	44	48	50	45
16.	1	2	13	16	16	15	1	13	45	50	Inv. 3, 45	58
17.	3	1	14	14	13	13	16	38	45	50	53	58
18.	2	3	15	16	14	14	35	24	43	43	30	Inv. 3, 46
19.	5	3	1	2	14	16	34	16	43	Inv. 1, 45	16	53
20.	1	10	3	3	17	1	30	2	Inv. 3	46	24	41

© Houghton Mifflin Harcourt Publishing Company

Saxon Math Intermediate 4 Homeschool Testing Book

Test Analysis Form–continued

Test Item No.	Test Number										
	13	**14**	**15**	**16**	**17**	**18**	**19**	**20**	**21**	**22**	**23**
	Lesson Assessed										
1.	Inv. 2	70	52	75	27	35	94	96	Inv. 6	101	94
2.	52	Inv. 5	61	57	57	88	92	Inv. 4	Inv. 6	101	111
3.	61	49	72	72	83	83	94	91	Inv. 6	95	Inv. 5
4.	Inv. 5	42, 59	72	70	Inv. 6	49	88	95	Inv. 6	102	Inv. 3, 70
5.	Inv. 3	35	72	79	Inv. 3, 70	59	Inv. 5	Inv. 3, 45	57	109	115
6.	59	70	49	74	81	23	Inv. 4	91	57	Inv. 4	103
7.	57	Inv. 1	74	77	42, 59	79	91	21, 69	Inv. 2	59	109
8.	63	63	Inv. 2	77	77	Inv. 2	93	Inv. 4	104	104	57
9.	Inv. 2	69	70	78	70	45	69, 70	93	103	49	83
10.	56	Inv. 2	Inv. 2, 69	31, 34	84	89	Inv. 3	57	83	72	88
11.	Inv. 5	Inv. 3	45	59	84	22	95	Inv. 2, Inv. 3	102	41	50, Inv. 3
12.	51	22	45, 50	52	22	52	60	34, 51	57, 60	50	91
13.	50	41	52	45	43	85	Inv. 4	94	41	91	107
14.	62	58	50	58	58	90	91	89	58	Inv. 3, 62	107
15.	62	67	58	50	85	80	86	22	86	67	114
16.	58	Inv. 3, 62	68	80	76	Inv. 3, 62	58	97	90	65	113
17.	65	68	71	76	45	50	90	98	105	105	80
18.	45, 47	62	41	41	41	86	80	86	62, 80	110	65
19.	50	50	24	24	2	24	76	90	45, 91	106	110
20.	41, 64	41, 64	Inv. 3, 62	40	67	2	2	76	16	Inv. 10	112

© Houghton Mifflin Harcourt Publishing Company

Test Analysis Form
Saxon Math Intermediate 4 Homeschool Testing Book

Answers

Test 1

1. **a.** ones   **b.** tens   **c.** hundreds
2. 438
3. 42, 48, 54
4. 18 wheels
5. 30 cents
6. 8
7. $235
8.
9. 32
10. 24
11. 45
12. 5 digits
13. 19
14. 19
15. 4
16. 4
17. 16
18. $n = 5$
19. 3 people
20. 9 problems

Test 2

1. 3 people
2. $88
3. 517
4. 330
5. nine hundred nineteen
6. six hundred nineteen
7. $3 + 4 = 7$ $7 - 4 = 3$
   $4 + 3 = 7$ $7 - 3 = 4$
8. **a.** hundreds   **b.** ones   **c.** tens
9. 7
10. $89
11. 30
12. 7
13. 9
14. 65

15. 3
16. 7
17. $5 + 3 + 1 + 4 = 13$
18. 18, 21, 24
19. 15, 12, 9
20. **B.** 352

Test 3

1. 93 students
2. 352
3. four hundred twenty-nine
4. $7 > 3$
5. $3 + 7 = 10$ $7 + 3 = 10$
   $10 - 3 = 7$ $10 - 7 = 3$
6. even
7. 7 coins
8. 40
9. $>$
10. $<$
11. 52
12. 24
13. 9
14. 17
15. 5
16. $716
17. 13
18. 17
19. 33
20. 6 digits

Test 4

1. 900 boats
2. $545
3. $400 + 9$
4. 8:12 p.m.
5. 72°F
6. $>$
7. $<$
8. 7 cm

Answers–continued

9. 60

10. $9

11. 6 people

12. 42 seashells

13. 147

14. 761

15. $27

16. 79

17. 28

18. 20

19. 1

20. 18 ×'s

Test 5

1. 17 dollars

2. **C.** 16

3. 181 people

4. 44 mm

5. 27, 36, 54

6. 3 feet

7. 40

8. <

9. 4:36 a.m.

10. Grand

11. $\frac{7}{12}$

12. 152

13. **A.**

14. $12.21

15. 15

16. 134

17. 759

18. 67

19. 842

20. 165

Test 6

1. 6 crayons

2. 152 boys

3. $29

4. nine hundred seven

5. 8 × 0 = 5 × 0

6. 5 cm

7. Sample:

8. $12

9. 42, 36, 18

10. 17 cm

11. 9:30 p.m.

12. 7 × 6

13. 200 cm

14. **C.** 9 × 5

15. 620

16. 47

17. 1,194

18. 51

19. 44

20. 50

Test 7

1. 105 miles

2. 874

3. Sample:

4. **a.** May   **b.** 1999

5. Sample:

6. 6 sq. cm

7. $\frac{5}{8}$

8. 6 × 5

9. 50 + 50 = 100

10. even

11. 175

12. **a.** 4   **b.** 49   **c.** 64

13. 9

14. 7

15. =

Answers–continued

16. 65

17. 333

18. four and two thirds

19. 6,000,000

20. 248

Test 8

1. $0.48

2. 132 miles

3. $2\frac{1}{4}$

4. =

5. 4 quarts

6. seven hundred twenty-four thousand, eight hundred sixty-eight

7. Sample:

8. 893 > 592

9. L

10. 16 inches

11. 90 + 80 = 170

12. 3 feet

13. $2\frac{2}{3}$

14. $1.37

15. 9

16. $895

17. **a.** 24   **b.** 32   **c.** 28

18. 369

19. 613

20. 36

Test 9

1. 338 tickets

2. $0.27

3. 400

4. Sample:

5. twelve and four tenths

6. 6:15 a.m.

7. $1\frac{3}{4}$ inches

8. $4\frac{5}{7}$

9. 685 cars

10. 839

11. 511

12. 9

13. $3.56

14. 180

15. 208

16. 100

17. 32

18. $10.90

19. 0.25

20. 11

Test 10

1. 1,177 students

2. 264 coins

3. **B.** 2 yards

4. 3

5. 3421

6. $3\frac{7}{8}$

7. 35 feet

8. 54 players

9. 500

10. 122,501

11. $3.69

12. 645

13. 951

14. 126

15. 511

16. 1.96

17. 6.94

18. $5.98

19. <

20. **a.** 9   **b.** 6   **c.** 7

Test 11

1. 6 weeks

2. 1, 3, 5, 15

3. 5 books

© Houghton Mifflin Harcourt Publishing Company

Answers
Saxon Math Intermediate 4 Homeschool Testing Book

Answers–continued

4. Sample: ⊕
5. 500 years
6. 30
7. <
8. 8 cm
9. 78 mm
10. 5,000
11. $6.65
12. 81,422
13. 28,569
14. 553
15. 18.47
16. 10
17. 7 R 3
18. 139
19. 951
20. 319

Test 12

1. 1,218
2. 245 people
3. 6 minutes
4. 5 apples
5. 360 miles
6. $\frac{5}{8}$
7. 1 century
8. <
9. 700
10. $\overline{TR}$ or $\overline{RT}$
11. 20
12. $88.20
13. 38,989
14. 2.44
15. 904
16. 3,800
17. 1,131
18. 1

19. 7 R 3
20. 7

Test 13

1. 18 feet
2. 51 beads
3. $\frac{3}{5}$
4. =
5. 144 sq. mm
6. 720
7. 196 miles
8. pentagon
9. 15 units
10. Sample: ▨□□ < ▨□□□
11. 73%
12. 154,481
13. $10.91
14. 160
15. 73
16. 2,244
17. 46
18. 8
19. 23.74
20. 13

Test 14

1. 24 posts
2. 65%
3. 735 raisins
4. 13,000
5. $1.87
6. 12 salespeople
7. −3
8. 13 sides
9. **a.** 4 cm **b.** 40 mm
10. 20 feet
11. 24 sq. feet
12. $631.16
13. $0.41

Answers–continued

14. $12.52

15. 480

16. 14

17. 69 R 3

18. 168

19. 1.36

20. 16

Test 15

1. 50 pages

2. $\frac{2}{5}$

3. 24 students

4. 24 students

5. pizza

6. 63 days

7. $\frac{2}{11}$

8. 5,000 meters

9. 2 kilometers

10. 73 mm

11. 32 mm

12. $3.41

13. 43,645

14. 8.89

15. $34.37

16. 56 R 5

17. 90 R 5

18. 60

19. 369

20. >

Test 16

1. **B.** south

2. $2.28

3. 54

4. 12 delegates

5.

6. $\frac{3}{7}$

7. 4,000 pounds

8. **A.** 300 grams

9. **B.**

10. $10,064

11. Sample: 1,000

12. 6 signs

13. 3,509

14. $55.79

15. 66.97

16. 807

17. 864 R 1

18. 41

19. 2,204

20. 2 cups in 1 pint < 4 cups in 1 quart

Test 17

1. 11:35 a.m.

2. 4 miles

3. **a.** $12.80   **b.** $7.20

4. 15 students

5. 12 square miles

6. **B.**

7. 7,000

8. 48 ounces

9. 6 roses

10. 0.435

11. $\frac{321}{1000}$

12. $57.22

13. 49.108

14. 4,347

15. 2,700

16. $0.91

17. 700

18. 80

19. 28

20. 2,010

© Houghton Mifflin Harcourt Publishing Company Saxon Math Intermediate 4 Homeschool Testing Book